SO-AIN-499

PEACEFUL
PROTESTERS

The White Rose Movement

Nonviolent Resistance to the Nazis

Bridey Heing

Cavendish Square

New York

Published in 2018 by Cavendish Square Publishing, LLC
243 5th Avenue, Suite 136, New York, NY 10016

Copyright © 2018 by Cavendish Square Publishing, LLC

First Edition

No part of this publication may be reproduced, stored in a retrieval system, or transmitted in any form or by any means—electronic, mechanical, photocopying, recording, or otherwise—without the prior permission of the copyright owner. Request for permission should be addressed to Permissions, Cavendish Square Publishing, 243 5th Avenue, Suite 136, New York, NY 10016. Tel (877) 980-4450; fax (877) 980-4454.

Website: cavendishsq.com

This publication represents the opinions and views of the author based on his or her personal experience, knowledge, and research. The information in this book serves as a general guide only. The author and publisher have used their best efforts in preparing this book and disclaim liability rising directly or indirectly from the use and application of this book.

All websites were available and accurate when this book was sent to press.

Library of Congress Cataloging-in-Publication Data

Names: Heing, Bridey, author.
Title: The White Rose movement : nonviolent resistance to the Nazis / Bridey Heing.
Description: New York : Cavendish Square Publishing, [2018] | Series: Peaceful protesters | Includes bibliographical references and index. | Identifiers: LCCN 2017017362 (print) | LCCN 2017019365 (ebook) | ISBN 9781502631206 (library bound) | ISBN 9781502633972 (Paperback) | ISBN 9781502631213 (E-book)
Subjects: LCSH: Weisse Rose (Resistance group)--Juvenile literature. | Anti-Nazi movement--Germany--Munich--Juvenile literature. | College students--Political activity--Germany--Munich--Juvenile literature. | Pamphlets--Germany--History--20th century--Juvenile literature.
Classification: LCC DD256.3 (ebook) | LCC DD256.3 .H377 2017 (print) | DDC 943.086--dc23
LC record available at https://lccn.loc.gov/2017017362

Editorial Director: David McNamara
Editor: Caitlyn Miller
Copy Editor: Nathan Heidelberger
Associate Art Director: Amy Greenan
Designer: Alan Sliwinski
Production Coordinator: Karol Szymczuk
Photo Research: J8 Media

The photographs in this book are used by permission and through the courtesy of: Cover, p. 44, 64 akg Images/Wittnstein/Newscom; p. 4 imageBROKER/Alamy Stock Photo; p. 8 Everett Historical/Shutterstock.com; p. 10 Corbis/Getty Images; p. 18, 46, 49, 50 Ullstein Bild/Getty Images; p. 21 Hulton Archive/Getty Images; p. 25 akg Images/Alamy Stock Photo; p. 26 Agencja Fotograficzna Caro/Alamy Stock Photo; p. 31 Universal Images Group/Alamy Stock Photo; p. 36 Itar-Tass Photo Agency/Alamy Stock Photo; p. 41 Keystone Pictures/Alamy Stock Photo; p. 51, 53 Interfoto/Alamy Stock Photo; p. 54-80 (background) Ekkasit Rakrotchit/Shutterstock.com; p. 80 Alan Copson City Pictures/Alamy Stock Photo; p. 84 Vlad Breazu/Alamy Stock Photo; p. 86 Bettmann/Getty Images; p. 92 Solodov Aleksey/Shutterstock.com; p. 98 United Archives Gmbh/Alamy Stock Photo; p. 102 Frank Boxler/AP Images.

Manufactured in China

CONTENTS

Memorials around Munich honor the legacy of the student-led White Rose movement, which confronted German silence in the face of Nazi crimes.

CHAPTER ONE

What Was the White Rose Movement?

Colleges and universities have long been hotbeds of dissent and efforts toward progress. Throughout history, students and their academic allies have challenged conventional thinking and oppression alike, creating groups that spread awareness and champion resistance. From protesting the Vietnam War to opposing dictatorships in the Middle East, educated and impassioned young people have been on the **vanguard** of speaking truth to power and changing their world.

In 1942, in the heart of **Nazi Germany**, that spirit of resistance spurred one of the most famous domestic movements against Adolf Hitler's government and **genocide**. The White Rose movement was founded by siblings Hans Scholl and Sophie Scholl, along with their friends, at the University of Munich. Most of the group's members were in their early twenties and had come of age under Hitler's regime. Although they had early on been part of Hitler's youth groups, the Scholls became disillusioned as they grew up and learned more about what the Nazi regime sought to do—namely the mass killing of Jewish citizens.

The Scholls and their friends decided to do what they could to undermine the German government and war machine by inspiring **nonviolent resistance** among German citizens. The White Rose movement printed pamphlets detailing the war crimes committed by Nazi forces and authorities, and they spread these pamphlets around campus. It is also believed that at the time of their arrest, the group's leadership was working to contact other resistance groups active in the country, but they were unable to do so before being caught in early 1943.

Sophie, Hans, and their fellow resistance member Christoph Probst were arrested in February 1943 while distributing pamphlets on campus. Later that month, the three were put on trial and found guilty of treason. Just hours later, they were executed by guillotine. According to officials who witnessed the execution, Sophie Scholl's last words were a call to action:

> *How can we expect righteousness to prevail when there is hardly anyone willing to give himself up individually to a righteous cause? Such a fine, sunny day, and I have to go, but what does my death matter, if through us, thousands of people are awakened and stirred to action?*

Shortly after their execution, the rest of the group's members were arrested, and many were executed. But their short-lived activism lives on today as an example of the bravery required to undertake nonviolent resistance in the face of tyranny. The White Rose movement is remembered as one of Nazi Germany's greatest detractors, and one of the many great youth resistance movements that has spurred change.

The Nazis

Nazi Germany is one of the best known and most highly documented oppressive regimes in modern history. Although Adolf Hitler ruled Germany for only twelve years, from 1933 to 1945, in that time he rallied support for a campaign of mass genocide and ethnic cleansing, launched a war that temporarily conquered much of Europe, and controlled his country through fear and intimidation. The shadow his memory, and that of the

Adolf Hitler joined what would become the Nazi Party after World War I.

people who supported him, casts over humanity is long and haunting, a constant reminder of the evils mankind is capable of.

Adolf Hitler was perhaps an unlikely leader, but in the aftermath of World War I, he brought together the support of enough dedicated followers to assure his power. A former soldier and failed artist, Hitler joined the **German Workers' Party** in 1919. He became the group's leader in 1921, by which time it had become the **National Socialist German Workers' Party**, commonly known as the Nazi Party. After a failed coup in 1923, he spent nine months in prison. It was then that he wrote *Mein Kampf*, a book that today is understood as a political manifesto highlighting the beliefs he eventually put into practice.

Hitler was able to rise to prominence in the years following his release due to widespread economic struggle. The **Treaty of Versailles**, which was negotiated in the aftermath of World War I, forced Germany to pay for the war that had decimated Europe. Hitler and others argued that these reparations were the source of economic downturn and out-of-control currency **hyperinflation** that had left many Germans destitute. By pairing a **populism** that spoke to Germany's economic insecurity with appeals to **anti-Semitism** and **nationalism**, Hitler reached a wide range of voters. In 1932, his Nazi Party won a large number of seats in the legislative **Reichstag**. As a result, Hitler became **chancellor** of Germany in 1933. Through a combination of legislation, staged terrorist attacks, and manipulation, Hitler became the sole ruler of Germany in 1934, declaring himself Führer and seizing all power.

Advocating a supposed need for *"Lebensraum,"* or "living space," Hitler gradually introduced a policy of genocide that killed millions. It is estimated that the Nazis killed around eleven million people as part of the Holocaust, their campaign of ethnic cleansing that targeted Jews, homosexuals, people living with disabilities, and **Roma** populations. The majority of their victims were Jewish, with around six million documented murders taking place at concentration camps and death camps across German-held territory. Other victims included prisoners of war (2.6 million Soviet prisoners died of hunger, while more were shot), innocent bystanders, and those who spoke out against Hitler and his regime.

Despite this danger, thousands within Germany fought back against the regime, with many giving their lives to try to defeat him.

Resistance to the Nazis

In countries like Greece, France, and Poland, there were united and organized resistance movements that undermined Nazi rule through various means, some of them violent. But in Germany, there was no such

The aftermath of a 1944 bombing that targeted Hitler. Such assassination attempts by internal resistance were unable to remove him from power.

The White Rose Movement: Nonviolent Resistance to the Nazis

overarching strategy of resistance, and instead movements were made up of smaller and largely independent groups with differing goals. Some hoped to stage a coup against Hitler by recruiting people close to him. A 1944 assassination attempt called the July Plot, or sometimes known as Operation Valkyrie, the code name for one part of the mission, failed. However, it highlights the growing disillusionment that had by that point taken root in Hitler's inner circle. Others engaged in sabotage, spying, and other activities that sought to undermine Nazi rule or inspire the full rejection of Nazi policy.

Resistance to Hitler was small but diverse, with resistance groups forming along political, religious, and social lines. Banned political parties like the Social Democrats and Communists, as well as politically motivated groups like anti-fascists, moved underground to help people flee the country or to spread anti-Nazi information. Religious groups also stood against Nazi policy, although they did not call for revolution or revolt. Churches were largely beyond Hitler's grasp when it came to cracking down on dissent. As such, priests and other Christian religious leaders were able to criticize the government to a certain extent. The Catholic clergy was among the earliest and strongest groups to oppose Hitler's policies, and Pope Pius XI wrote a 1937 encyclical called "With Burning Concern." Read from every Catholic pulpit in Germany, it was highly critical of Hitler's treatment of the church, minorities, and other persecuted groups. Pius also wrote against the nationalism that had gripped Germany, and which Hitler advocated:

> *Whoever exalts race, or the people, or the State, or a particular form of State, or the depositories of power, or any other fundamental value of the human community—however necessary and honorable be their function in worldly things—whoever raises these notions above their standard value and divinizes them to an idolatrous level, distorts and perverts an order of the world planned and created by God; he is far from the true faith in God and from the concept of life which that faith upholds.*

There was also resistance within the military, with some inside the Foreign Office and army working with spies or outside groups to share intelligence with allies. They also conspired against Hitler in attempts to overthrow him. Alongside these organized groups were average Germans who worked alone to hide Jews or help them escape the country.

Although resistance to the Nazis was widespread, it was also small. The majority of Germans either agreed with Hitler, did not know what was taking place, or decided to not get involved in efforts to combat Nazism. While today it is easy to cast judgment on those who chose to stay on the sidelines, speaking out came with very real dangers. Around seventy-seven thousand people were executed following trials in Nazi courts, while thousands of others are believed to have been sent to concentration camps or targeted by the **Gestapo**, or the Secret State Police.

Nonviolent Resistance in Nazi Germany

One of the questions that resisters were faced with from the earliest days of Nazi power was how best to counter the regime. Faced with such a blatantly violent government that had proved its willingness to kill, many chose to coordinate bombings, assassination attempts, and more.

Nonviolent resistance was common among those who chose to speak and act against the Nazi regime, but often it was invisible. This included gathering intelligence or helping people flee persecution. Given the high costs of making your opposition to Hitler known (which could include arrest, torture, or execution) it is no wonder that so few were willing to risk their lives. The Scholls' own father, Robert, spent four months in prison in 1942 for saying to a coworker who asked about the war, "The war! It is already lost. This Hitler is God's scourge on mankind, and if the war doesn't end soon, the Russians will be sitting in Berlin."

This is in part why the White Rose group is so unique. Through leaflets and graffiti around Munich, members of the group were outspokenly and publicly defiant of Hitler's policies at a time when it would almost certainly result in their deaths. Hans and Sophie Scholl's sister Inge said after their death:

> *We were living in a society where despotism, hate, and lies had become the normal state of affairs. Every day that you were not in jail was like a gift. No one was safe from arrest for the slightest unguarded remark, and some disappeared forever for no better reason ... Hidden ears seemed to be listening to everything that was being spoken in Germany. The terror was at your elbow wherever you went.*

Despite the risk, the Scholls and the White Rose decided to act. After becoming disillusioned with the Nazi vision for Germany, Hans and Sophie became increasingly politically outspoken until finally they could wait no longer. Elisabeth Scholl, Hans and Sophie's sister, felt her siblings understood what they were getting into when they started. During his trial, Hans said, "I knew what I took upon myself and I was prepared to lose my life by so doing." Elisabeth later wrote:

> *We learned in the spring of 1942 of the arrest and execution of ten or twelve Communists. And my brother said, "In the name of civic and Christian courage something must be done." Sophie knew the risks. [Sophie's boyfriend] Fritz Hartnagel told me about a conversation in May 1942. Sophie asked him for a thousand marks but didn't want to tell him why. He warned her that resistance could cost both her head and her neck. She told him, "I'm aware of that." Sophie wanted the money to buy a printing press to publish the anti-Nazi leaflets.*

Between June 1942 and February 1943, White Rose printed and handed out thousands of pamphlets that called the German people to action against Hitler. Crimes committed by the Nazis were detailed in each of the brief tracts, and they stirred moral sentiment. The third leaflet read in part, "Why do you allow these men who are in power to rob you step by step, openly and in secret, of one domain of your rights after another, until one day nothing, nothing at all will be left but a mechanized state system presided over by criminals and drunks? Is your spirit already so crushed by abuse that you forget it is your right—or rather, your moral duty—to eliminate this system?"

The Scholls were joined by Christoph Probst, Alexander Schmorell, Professor Kurt Huber, Willi Graf, and others who supported their work with money, resources, or by handing out their materials. The group also graffitied anti-Nazi imagery and wording around Munich, including the word "Freedom" and the phrase "Down with Hitler."

Shortly before starting the group, Hans wrote, "What are we going to have to show in the way of resistance—as compared to the Communists, for instance—when this terror is over? We will be standing there empty-handed. We will have no answer when we are asked: What did you do about it?"

The answer, as it turned out, was a legacy of heroism in the face of tyranny. But sadly, he and his sister would not live to see the end of Hitler's terror.

The Legacy of the White Rose

Although their reach was short during their lives, the work of the White Rose movement was of immediate importance. Allied forces dropped copies of their sixth and final leaflet across Germany, and support for the group was swift following the executions of the Scholls and Probst. Thomas Mann, a German author living in exile and the host of a BBC radio show, said of the movement in June 1943: "Good, splendid young people! You shall not have died in vain; you shall not be forgotten."

Thomas Mann was right; even today, we remember this brief and powerful movement as one of Germany's greatest resistance groups. Monuments, including Scholl Siblings Square and Professor Huber Square near the University of Munich, stand in the city where they tried to bring about change. Films, books, and operas have been written to honor the group, and one of the country's top literary prizes is named for the Scholls. By breaking what had been a near code of silence surrounding discontent with Nazi policy, the White Rose movement was able to shake the regime to its very core and make clear that although the people were afraid to speak out, unhappiness and disapproval were spreading. Despite being young, they were brave, selfless, and uncowed by efforts to intimidate them. No matter what, they were going to ensure that their voices were heard. It was a fact that they made clear during their trial, when they stated that although they were alone in their actions, in spirit they did not feel alone. Sophie said, "Somebody, after all, had to make a start. What we wrote and said is also believed by many others. They just don't dare express themselves as we did."

Adolf Hitler rose to power through manipulation, staged terrorism, and genuine support.

CHAPTER TWO

A Threat Rises in Germany

T he White Rose movement emerged from a particular moment in a very unique period of history. Multiple years into Adolf Hitler's reign in Germany and at a point in World War II when many had started to question the validity of the conflict and Hitler's own ambitions, the Scholls and their friends were emblematic of a changing perspective. But they were still in the minority, and most Germans did not share their conviction. There are many reasons why, as we will see below, and many are rooted in both continued support for Adolf Hitler and fear of his government.

Fennville District Library
400 West Main Street
Fennville MI 49408
fennvilledl.michlibrary.org

World War I

Although World War I ended over a decade before Hitler rose to power in Germany, it played a crucial role in setting the stage for the spread of Nazism. The First World War began in 1914, following the declaration of war between Austria-Hungary and Serbia after the assassination of Austrian Archduke Franz Ferdinand. Due to complex alliances between other European states, almost every country in Europe and some in North Africa and Asia were drawn into the war almost immediately. The United States did not join the war until 1917. Germany was one of the Central powers aligned with Austria-Hungary, the Ottoman Empire, and others. France, Russia, and Great Britain fought as the Allied powers with several other states, including Italy and Japan. Russia left the war in 1917 following the overthrow of the monarchy there.

Fighting ended in a ceasefire in 1918, by which time the international order was completely reformed. The war was the first to use trench warfare and modern weaponry. This led to a staggering death rate of around seventeen million across both military and civilian populations. An additional twenty million were injured. The political makeup of Europe and much of the world changed dramatically following the conflict's end. The Ottoman Empire, which controlled the Middle East and parts of North Africa, was dissolved, and France and Great Britain divided its territory into the countries we know today. The German Empire was also dissolved, although the country retained its territorial integrity for the most part. The Austro-Hungarian Empire collapsed, and in Russia the former Czarist Empire dissolved and was reformed into the Soviet Union. In just four short years, the balance of power and rule of empire was almost rewritten completely.

Germany was declared one of the aggressors in the war and was made to assume responsibility for all "loss and damage," according to the Treaty of Versailles, which formally ended the war in 1919. As part of Germany's taking on that responsibility, the country was made to

The signing of the Treaty of Versailles. The treaty levied harsh penalties against Germany.

disarm fully, give up territory, and pay an estimated 132 billion marks (the 2017 equivalent of $442 billion) to countries like France and Great Britain. The amount Germany was to repay was criticized by economists as too much, and it would become the bedrock of Hitler's gradual climb to power.

In Germany, a sense of betrayal swept the country in the years after the war as people believed the German forces could have prevailed. Although this was impossible by the end of the war, this sense of distrust in the establishment and belief that it turned its back on the soldiers was a driving force in the political changes to come. Hitler himself, in a military hospital recovering from being temporarily blinded by mustard gas at the time of the surrender, was among those who felt immense anger over the decision, writing in *Mein Kampf*:

> **"**
>
> *Everything went black before my eyes; I tottered and groped my way back to the ward, threw myself on my bunk, and dug my burning head into my blanket and pillow. So it had all been in vain. In vain all the sacrifices and privations; in vain the hours in which, with mortal fear clutching at our hearts, we nevertheless did our duty; in vain the death of two million who died. Had they died for this? Did all this happen only*

so that a gang of wretched criminals could lay hands on the Fatherland? I knew that all was lost. Only fools, liars and criminals could hope for mercy from the enemy. In these nights hatred grew in me, hatred for those responsible for this deed. Miserable and degenerate criminals! The more I tried to achieve clarity on the monstrous events in this hour, the more the shame of indignation and disgrace burned my brow.

As the German Empire fell, it was replaced by the democratic Weimar Republic, a representative federal republic with a newly written constitution and a balance of powers between the Reichstag, a chancellor, and an elected president.

But the Weimar Republic was besieged with problems. Hyperinflation set in shortly after the war as the country printed more and more currency, and strikes started taking place across the country. Over the course of 1923, German marks became effectively useless. A single loaf of bread, which had cost around 250 marks in January of that year, cost around 200 billion marks by that November. Currency values were changing on an hourly basis, and some people used the currency as fuel because it was worth so little. While a small group of people were able to make a profit, most people were living under extreme hardship with currency that could hardly buy them food.

This economic struggle, combined with the sense of distrust in the Weimar government, made ideal circumstances for political extremism. In 1923, nationalists, Communists, and other political groups began agitating around the country. And a group of fascists called the Nazis attempted to stage a revolt in Munich. Although in 1924 the economy began to stabilize and Germany saw progress toward rebuilding its strength, the 1929 stock market crash plunged the country back into hardship. Five years later, Adolf Hitler was in power.

The Rise of Adolf Hitler

Adolf Hitler was born in Austria and spent his adolescence in Vienna. After the death of his mother in 1907, he spent years living in homeless shelters and hostels, where he was exposed to growing racism and anti-Semitism that was spreading around the city. Populist leaders rallied support using nationalism and fear of immigrants, as well as pan-Germanism. In his own writings, Hitler called his time in Vienna instrumental in shaping his political views, although some who knew him at a younger age later said he was already anti-Semitic as a young man.

At the start of World War I in 1914, Hitler volunteered for the Bavarian army, despite his being an Austrian. This should have disqualified him, but instead he was sent to the western front as a dispatch runner. At the

Hitler (*right*) fought for Germany during World War I.

Battle of the Somme, he was wounded and received a medal for bravery. This was the first of three decorations awarded to him over the course of the war.

After the war, Hitler went to Munich and joined the German Workers' Party, which would eventually become the National Socialist German Workers' Party, or the Nazi Party. When he joined in 1919, it was a small group, but membership grew rapidly as Hitler began giving public speeches. In 1921, he temporarily resigned from the party and said he would only rejoin if he was made chairman. A vote was held that July, and he replaced the former chairman by near unanimous approval.

In 1923, Hitler staged what has become known as the **Beer Hall Putsch**, an attempt to bring about a revolt. At a beer hall in Munich, Hitler and some of his supporters disrupted a public meeting organized by a political leader, and they declared that a revolution had begun. Yet they hadn't taken hold of the government buildings they had claimed to, and within three days, Hitler was arrested and charged with high treason. Although sentenced to five years in prison, he served only nine months of his sentence and was released in late 1924. While in prison, he wrote his book, *Mein Kampf,* which was published the following year and in a second edition in 1926.

Although Hitler tried to reorganize the Nazi Party after leaving prison, it wasn't until the crash of 1929 that their extremist politics became popular. The stock market crash that year left millions out of work and resulted in the collapse of banks, destroying the economic progress that had been made since 1924. Once again fear, racism, and distrust of the government surfaced, and Hitler was positioned perfectly to manipulate those emotions for his own political gain. Numerous factors came together to help Hitler, including support from industrialists who

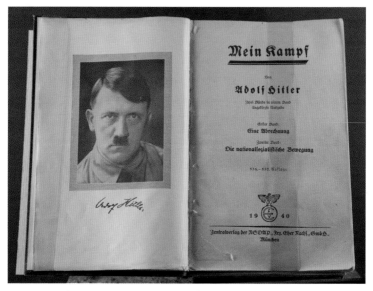

Mein Kampf was Hitler's political manifesto, written during his time in prison following the failed Beer Hall Putsch.

feared communism could overtake Germany. At the same time, Hitler was using propaganda to spread his message to communities by using very specific targeted slogans, and his **SA** forces were physically intimidating opponents. Hitler's speaking skills helped him whip crowds into a frenzy and draw more and more followers, while his bigoted speeches about so-called Jewish conspiracies fed the sense of victimization that pushed him closer and closer to power.

Running on a platform of rejecting the Treaty of Versailles's reparations and growing the economy while adding jobs, Hitler was able to more than double the number of votes the Nazi Party received in national elections, from 2.6 percent in 1928 to 18.3 percent in 1930 and 37.3 percent in 1932, when Hitler himself ran for the presidency. Although he did not win that election, President Paul von Hindenburg did agree to name him chancellor in January 1933. Along with his appointment, his supporters Wilhelm Frick became minister of the interior and Hermann Goering became minister of the interior for Prussia at Hitler's insistence.

In February 1933, the Reichstag was set on fire, and Hitler's ally Goering quickly blamed Communists. However, historians disagree about whether the fire was set by the accused Marinus van der Lubbe or Hitler's supporters. The fire marked a turning point for Hitler and the Nazi Party, which won over 40 percent in the elections held that March. With the highest number of seats in parliament but not the majority, Hitler had to manipulate the legislature to pass the Enabling Act, which granted him emergency powers for four years. By arresting all Communists in the legislature and keeping out several Social Democrats, the Nazis were able to secure enough votes to pass the bill according to procedure. Germany had effectively become a dictatorship. And yet, according to the American journalist William Shirer, even as late as 1935 Hitler's popularity was vast. Writing of the 1935 Nazi Party Rally in Nuremberg, Shirer said:

> *Like a Roman emperor Hitler rode into this medieval town at sundown today past solid phalanxes of wildly cheering Nazis who packed the narrow streets ... For the life of me I could not quite comprehend what hidden springs he undoubtedly unloosed in the hysterical mob which was greeting him so wildly ... I got caught in a mob of ten thousand hysterics who jammed the moat in front of Hitler's hotel, shouting, "We want our Führer." I was a little shocked at the faces, especially those of the women, when Hitler finally appeared on the balcony for a moment ... They looked up at him as if he were a Messiah.*

Domestic Oppression Grows

Today we know that Hitler's ultimate goals were genocide and domination. Once he had secured almost total power he moved gradually to repress the rights of Germans. He banned opposition parties and intimidated others into breaking up. At the same time, he put his own supporters into positions of power and replaced powerful groups like trade unions with organizations that were beholden to the Nazi Party. Rights like freedom of the press or freedom of speech were effectively abolished. The Nazis also started passing laws targeting Jewish citizens. By July 1933, the Nazi Party was the only legal party in the country, and between June 30 and July 2, 1934, Hitler targeted potential threats from within the SA during the Night of the Long Knives, which resulted in the deaths of several SA leaders and other political opponents. Hindenburg, who was still president at this time, died in August 1934. Rather than holding new elections, the government passed a law combining the positions of chancellor and president, making Hitler the country's sole executive.

Between 1933 and 1939, more than four hundred regulations were introduced to take rights away from Jews in Germany. The earliest was in 1933, with the Law for the Restoration of the Professional Civil Service, which barred Jewish citizens and those deemed "politically unreliable" from working in state service. Laws that followed barred

Jews from universities, medical professions, and practicing law. In 1935, Hitler introduced the Nuremberg Laws, two laws that stripped Jews, and later people of color and Roma, of rights. Under the laws, Aryans and these persecuted groups were not allowed to intermarry, and all non-Aryans lost their citizenship. Between 1937 and 1938, laws were passed that took away property and businesses from Jewish families and workers and sold them at a cheap price to Nazi officials.

Kristallnacht, or the Night of Broken Glass, took place on November 9 and 10 in 1938. It involved the widespread destruction and defacement of Jewish businesses, places of worship, and neighborhoods. In its aftermath, thirty thousand Jewish men were arrested and sent to concentration camps, the first such large-scale incarceration of Jews during the Nazi regime. It marked a turning point for domestic repression. A wave of anti-Jewish legislation followed, along with the widespread deportation and murder of Jewish populations.

Other domestic oppression was carried out during this time as well, including euthanasia programs that targeted the mentally disabled, those with hereditary illnesses, the physically disabled, and others. The state carried out waves of killings between 1939 and 1945, first targeting children and later adults. It is believed that around 260,000 people were murdered as part of these programs.

Kristallnacht, or the Night of Broken Glass, was a violent turning point in Hitler's targeting of Jews.

For those who the Nazi government did not target for deportation or murder, life revolved around the Nazi Party. Propaganda was widespread and replaced other forms of media, inundating the public with pro-Hitler messages through film, art, and rallies. Education was reformed to focus on Nazi-approved lessons, including those of racial biology and physical fitness to pave the way for military service. History was of a particular concern for Hitler as a way to control a country's narrative. He wrote in *Mein Kampf*:

"

The subject matter of our historical teaching must be curtailed. The chief value of that teaching is to make the principal lines of historical development understood. The more our historical teaching is

limited to this task, the more we may hope that
it will turn out subsequently to be of advantage
to the individual and, through the individual, to
the community as a whole. For history must not
be studied merely with a view to knowing what
happened in the past but as a guide for the future,
and to teach us what policy would be the best to
follow for the preservation of our own people.

All in the civil service and military had to swear loyalty not to the country of Germany but to Hitler himself, a dangerous precedent that made Hitler the highest power in the land. Rights like a fair trial and freedom of expression were no longer respected, and even those who merely spoke out against the Nazis could face imprisonment. Meanwhile, Hitler's Brownshirts, **SS**, and Gestapo ruled the streets with terror.

World War II

In 1935, Hitler began the process of reunifying Germany and drawing German-speaking territories under German authority. That year, a territory on the southwest border with France called Saarland voted to join Germany rather than stay under control of the League of Nations. The next year, Hitler sent forces into the Rhineland to reoccupy the demilitarized area in the west, marking a violation of the

Treaty of Versailles and the first military action leading up to World War II. Both Great Britain and France responded with appeasement rather than military action, a choice that would be remembered as a mistake. In 1938, Hitler annexed Austria and the Sudetenland area of Czechoslovakia, a region with an ethnically German majority.

September 1, 1939, is generally accepted as the start of World War II in Europe (although it began in 1937 in the Pacific with the start of the Second Sino-Japanese War). On that September day, Hitler invaded Poland. Two days later, France and Britain formally declared war on Germany. The following year, German troops invaded Denmark and Norway, and then France. In July 1940, the German Luftwaffe began carrying out bombings in Britain, including aerial raids on London. In 1941, the Soviet Union entered the war following German attacks on Soviet territory. In late 1941, the United States was attacked by German ally Japan, and after the US declared war in retaliation, Germany formally declared war on the United States. Less than a decade after Hitler took power in Germany, the Second World War was truly global.

By its end in 1945, the war would involve one hundred million troops from more than thirty countries and would draw resources from every part of the world while causing widespread destruction in Europe and the Pacific. In addition to the millions killed during the Holocaust and the estimated one million killed during bombings on large population centers like Hiroshima and Dresden, as many as eighty-five million were killed during the war through fighting and from starvation or disease. Some estimates place the dead at sixty million, which would be around 3 percent of the world's population circa 1940.

During the early years of the war, the German advance seemed unstoppable. The military used effective maneuvers to both conquer and hold territory, while carrying out their program of genocide and ethnic cleansing in the areas they held. This allowed Hitler to use the war to his advantage and gain support from Germans. As they saw it, he was following through on his promises to make Germany a great power once again. Although it is not clear how much Germans knew about the atrocities being carried out, at this time soldiers and those in the military did know about the Holocaust and the brutality German forces showed to civilians and prisoners of war. Resistance existed at this time, mostly in the form of spy networks that leaked information about military strategy to the Allies. By 1941, Hans and Sophie Scholl had joined civilians who were questioning the motives behind the war and whether or not German victory was good for mankind. That year, Sophie wrote to her boyfriend at the eastern front that she would not help collect winter coats for the soldiers because she refused to help Germany win the war. "We must lose the war," she wrote as winter began to overtake the German troops moving into Russia.

As it happened, one year later the eastern front would prove crucial in reversing the course of the German army.

The Tide Turns

The Battle of Stalingrad is often considered the turning point of World War II, when Hitler's war machine stalled and the Allies were able to make crucial inroads. During the winter between 1942 and 1943, the German army moved toward and entered the Russian city of Stalingrad. But while they fought bitterly, the German army was unable to capture the city—street by street, the Russians and Germans continuously took areas and lost them. In November 1942, the Russian army gained the upper hand and trapped the German forces as winter set in. The situation for the German soldiers was dire as food ran low and the cold became deadly, with one writing:

> *My hands are done for, and have been ever since the beginning of December. The little finger of my left hand is missing and—what's even worse—the three middle fingers of my right one are frozen. I can only hold my mug with my thumb and little finger. I'm pretty helpless; only when a man has lost any fingers does he see how much he needs them for the smallest jobs. The best*

thing I can do with the little finger is to shoot with it. My hands are finished.

But Hitler refused to give up. He wrote to Commander Friedrich Paulus in late January 1943:

" ....

> *Surrender is forbidden. 6 Army will hold their positions to the last man and the last*

Brutal fighting and harsh Russian winter characterized the Battle of Stalingrad, with German forces surrendering to Russian troops in 1943.

The White Rose Movement: Nonviolent Resistance to the Nazis

round and by their heroic endurance will make an unforgettable contribution towards the establishment of a defensive front and the salvation of the Western world.

He wasn't wrong that the army would hold their position, although the salvation of the Western world was perhaps shaped by the eventual *defeat* of Germany at Stalingrad. Just a few days after Hitler sent that communication to Paulus, the commander surrendered the troops under his command, and two days later the general in charge of the other half of the forces surrendered as well. By that time, around 250,000 German forces had died from fighting, starvation, or the cold. Around 550,000 were wounded or captured.

At that point, the war's momentum turned to the Allies. In the Pacific, Mediterranean, and Atlantic theaters, Allied forces were able to undermine Germany and Japan's success and begin offensive measures. By mid-1944, D-Day had taken place and the Allies liberated Paris, a hugely significant military victory and symbolic moment that boosted morale after years of fighting. At the same time, the Soviet Union began offensive attacks along the eastern front, pushing Germany out of Ukraine and eastern Poland. On April 30, 1945, Soviet forces entered Berlin. That same day, Hitler and some of his closest allies killed themselves in his underground bunker, where he had spent the final days of the war. Nazi Germany was no more.

Life Under the Nazi Regime

One of the great questions of the twentieth century and into today is how Germany, a democratic and diverse country, was able to be overtaken by a tyrant. Immediately after the Second World War, many believed Hitler had seized power essentially by force, with little true support from the German people. However, we now know that it had far more to do with complacency and a willingness to "go along" with his rule, combined with a fear of taking action against him. The answer is complex, and in some respects, even today, we struggle to understand the factors that led to Hitler's rise. But looking at life in Nazi Germany can offer some insight, and it can provide a deeper understanding of the world in which the White Rose developed and why their work was so remarkably brave.

As we've seen, Hitler's rise to power was enabled by multiple factors, from the widespread unpopularity of the Treaty of Versailles to distrust of the Weimar Republic. He was also able to play on economic hardship and the sense of victimhood that gripped postwar Germany, combining it with a latent anti-Semitism that was common in cities across Germany. These themes, along with his keen sense of the power of propaganda and his uniquely striking speaking skills, made it easy for him to gain followers. This was something he understood well. In *Mein Kampf*, written in 1924, Hitler wrote:

> " ....
>
> *The masses find it difficult to understand politics, their intelligence is small. Therefore all effective propaganda must be limited to a very few points. The masses will only remember only the simplest ideas repeated a thousand times over. If I approach the masses with reasoned arguments, they will not understand me. In the mass meeting, their reasoning power is paralyzed. What I say is like an order given under hypnosis.*

Hitler's rise to power was also cloaked heavily in legality, and he was adept at using procedure to obscure the rapid consolidation of power he undertook. By combining the use of emergency powers with intimidation by his secret police and **paramilitary** units, Hitler moved quickly but seemingly according to reason. He and his government passed laws (albeit through a hindered legislature) that gave his programs of genocide and repression an appearance of officiality. Hitler also used the threat of criminals and potential sabotage against the German nation to justify the introduction of early concentration camps and slave labor.

In order to control the population of Germany that he sought to win over to Nazism, he used both fear and manipulation. Hitler's security apparatus targeted those he saw as potential rivals and those it identified as being "racially inferior," but to gain support, they positioned these moves as being related to national security. At the same time, Hitler played on fears of communism and deep-seated anti-Semitism to win over followers. As a result, those who did not agree with him were either targeted for reprisal or stayed quiet out of fear of being turned in to the state. In his book *Hitler's Compromises: Coercion and Consensus in Nazi Germany*, Nathan Stoltzfus writes:

" ·

> *Nazi compromise and terror were not pitted against each other in toe-to-toe opposition but deployed in mutual support to manage the people's thinking and values. Upon coming to power, the Nazi Party jailed, tortured, and intimidated the leaders of rival political parties, a brutality that was not just tolerated but also encouraged by millions and millions of Germans, due to widespread popular anti-communism. Many Germans saw the Nazi terror against Jews and leaders on the Left as rightly targeting the nation's troublemakers, and the dictatorship*

also sought and received popular acceptance in ostracizing those it identified as social outsiders.

For young people, including the Scholls, indoctrination was key for Hitler's goals. Inge, the eldest of the Scholls,

Youth groups that advocated Nazi ideology were an important part of Hitler's social program, which aimed at instilling Nazi beliefs from a young age.

ENABLING ACT

Hitler's government passed hundreds of decrees and pieces of legislation that radically changed the course of German society. But the first and perhaps most important was the Enabling Act of 1933, which gave Hitler nearly unlimited power. Passed in the aftermath of the Reichstag Fire and an election that saw Hitler's Nazi Party take just shy of a majority of seats in the legislature, the law's journey through government was a hint at what Hitler was capable of. By that time, he had amassed significant support and authority as chancellor despite still serving under President Hindenburg. But on March 23, 1933, Hitler moved to ensure he was given near total power by introducing to a session of the parliament a bill called "The Law to Remedy the Distress of People and Reich." The bill gave the cabinet (essentially made up of Hitler's supporters) power to introduce new laws without bringing them to the parliament first and to do so without the approval of the president, allowing Hitler and his team to bypass all checks and balances on their legislative authority.

He didn't have enough votes with just his own party, so to ensure it would pass, Hitler made deals with politically centrist parties and nationalist parties. At the same time, he arrested members of the Communist Party and used his paramilitary to ensure Social Democrats, who would certainly vote against it, weren't able to make it to the vote. In the end, the Enabling Act passed 444 to 94. It was the first step on Hitler's rise to ultimate power in Germany—and it was done technically legally, setting the stage for further abuses of procedure and law under his rule.

wrote about what was so alluring about the Nazi program for young people when she wrote of her time in the German League of Girls. Inge recalled a sense of excitement, community, and common purpose that proved irresistible. But her writing also belies the idea that no one knew what was happening at the hands of the Nazis. When one girl in her camp unit raised concerns about the Nuremberg Laws in 1935, the girls were allowed to talk about it but were then distracted the next day.

Illusion was an important part of how Hitler came to and maintained power in Germany, but it didn't last forever. The story of the White Rose, and the political evolution of the Scholl siblings, shows that.

Hans and Sophie Scholl were students at the University of Munich when they decided to found the White Rose movement.

CHAPTER THREE

Nonviolent Resistance

Though brief, the White Rose is today remembered as one of the most powerful and symbolic resistance movements in Nazi Germany. They have become emblematic of how young people saw the actions of the Nazi regime and how Germans were beginning to understand the atrocities being carried out. But the road from college students to resistance heroes was not an easy one for the Scholls. Like many young people, they were initially supportive of Hitler and even took part in Hitler Youth groups in their hometown. They quickly became disillusioned, however, and began looking for ways they could manifest their resistance.

Alexander Schmorell met Hans Scholl while studying medicine at the University of Munich and became a member of the White Rose.

That chance came at the University of Munich, where Hans met fellow medical students like Alexander Schmorell and Christoph Probst, who had also been to the battlefield and learned of the widespread killings that were taking place. That, combined with their understanding of Hitler's repressive policies, drove them to take action as the White Rose, which would eventually find them all charged with treason and sentenced to death.

The Scholls' Political Evolution

Hans and Sophie Scholl were raised in Ulm, Germany, with their siblings Inge, Elisabeth, Werner, and Thilde. Their father was liberal and opposed the Nazis as soon as they began rising to power. The siblings did not immediately reject National Socialism, but being raised in a household where politics was discussed frequently and openly surely shaped Hans and Sophie, laying the foundation on which their own resistance would be built.

Despite disagreeing with them, Robert Scholl allowed his children to express themselves and eventually join the

Hitler Youth. Elisabeth later recalled that they didn't give their father's words much weight in the matter, recounting that they were excited about the Hitler Youth.

They weren't alone. By 1933, when Hans Scholl joined, the Hitler Youth had around one hundred thousand participants, and membership eventually became compulsory. The girls joined Bund Deutscher Mädel, a girls' version of the boys' Hitler Youth. The programs included physical exercises and projects similar to modern scouting organizations, but with added ideological indoctrination. Inge Scholl later remembered how drawn the kids were to it, which was in part due to the communal aspect of the program:

"

> But there was something else that drew us with mysterious power and swept us along: the closed ranks of marching youth with banners waving, eyes fixed straight ahead, keeping time to drumbeat and song. Was not this sense of fellowship overpowering? It is not surprising that all of us, Hans and Sophie and the others, joined the Hitler Youth. We entered into it with body and soul, and we could not understand why our father did not approve, why he was not happy and proud. On the contrary, he was quite displeased with us.

For Hans, who was quickly approaching the age at which he could join the military, his support for Hitler went further. He seems to have believed more stridently in the ideology of the Nazi Party than his siblings, even defending Hitler to his father. This support wasn't rare, even outside of Germany. War-torn Europe was still recovering from World War I in the early 1930s, and many supported Hitler's stated goal of rebuilding the economy and his strident tone against the Allies who had defeated Germany earlier in the century. To be clear, Hitler and his government were anti-Semitic and nationalist from their earliest days. Yet many people around the world wanted to believe that he would moderate his message once he solidified power. Even in England, where opposition to Hitler during the war would eventually sweep the country, Hitler had support from politicians and aristocrats alike who saw him as a strong leader who would possibly lead Germany to prosperity. Many feared the rise of communism in the Soviet Union under Joseph Stalin more than they feared the rise of fascism in Germany, and for them a strong Germany was protection from the creeping influence of the Soviet Union.

But like so many others, Hans was disillusioned quickly. In 1936, just three years after he had excitedly joined the Hitler Youth, he was asked to be a flag bearer at Hitler's Nuremberg Rally. Although he was at first thrilled at the honor, the event marked a turning point in how

Like many others, Hans Scholl was at first a strong supporter of Hitler. But that changed as he came to understand the true nature of the Nazi government.

he saw Hitler's ideology and policy. When he returned home, he was no longer enamored of Hitler.

Around that time, the rest of his siblings started seeing the Nazi regime for what it was, too. One of his sisters recalled the gradual realization that Hitler and his government had dangerous plans, and how they saw it affecting their own communities, especially when Jewish students were forced out of schools.

After his experience at the Nuremberg Rally, Hans began pulling away from the Nazi program and decided to start his own youth group. By that time, membership in the Hitler Youth was required by law, and it was illegal to take part in any youth programs other than the Hitler Youth. Although it may seem strange, it was an important part of Nazi indoctrination. Children are often more easily manipulated and influenced than adults. By making sure that they were exposed to Nazi ideology from a young age, the government was able to ensure that the next generation would grow up without even questioning their beliefs. A similar strategy is used by groups today, including ISIS.

But Hans decided to start a group anyway, and at age nineteen he rallied his friends to start taking part in adventures around Ulm. Hans and his friends hiked, camped, and sang and wrote songs. Innocent though it may sound, Hans and his friends were undermining some of the most central tenets of Nazi ideology, replacing Nazi ritual and propaganda with their own chants and songs, well outside the traditional German ones Hitler and his team preferred young people to learn. They were also putting themselves in danger, along with their families. Shortly after the group started meeting, Inge, Sophie, and their brother Werner were arrested on suspicion of taking part in activities outside of the Hitler Youth.

As a teenager, Sophie Scholl was arrested for taking part in non-Hitler Youth activities. Her arrest was a personal turning point in how she saw the regime.

Although they were released shortly after, for Sophie it was a turning point, much like the Nuremberg Rally was for her brother. The Nazi regime failed to see that Sophie, then sixteen years old, would eventually pose a threat to them, and they let her go. But the damage had been done.

Sophie's growing alienation could be seen in letters she wrote to her boyfriend, Fritz

Hartnagel, a soldier in the German army. Her letters to him were critical of the Nazis and highlighted her changing views of where the country was headed.

Starting the White Rose

Christoph Probst was a key member of the White Rose.

In the early 1940s, Hans was a medical student at the University of Munich. Along with other medical students, he was sent to aide the medical corps traveling with the German army into France. He spent those months observing the horrors of war and learning more about what was taking place in other parts of German territory, such as the killing of Russian prisoners of war and the genocide of the Jews.

When he returned to the University of Munich, Hans had already met Alex Schmorell and George Wittenstein, two of the people who would go on to join the White Rose. Schmorell, who was later made a saint by the Orthodox Church, was from a wealthy family and used his allowance to buy supplies for the group. He grew tired of talk and urged his friends to start taking action, saying, "What are we waiting for? Until the war is over and everybody points to us and says we tolerated such a regime without protest?"

Wittenstein later wrote about his time with the White Rose, noting that what they were doing was very rare at the time:

> *Organized resistance was practically impossible. One could not speak openly, even with close friends, never knowing whether they might not be Nazi spies or collaborators. So well organized was the control and surveillance by the party, that each city block had a party functionary assigned to spy on his neighbors. This "Blockwart" was ostensibly responsible for the well being of the residents of his city block, but in reality had to monitor, record and report on activities, conversations, and remarks of each person, as well as on their associations. Even the privacy of one's home was not assured: a tea cozy or pillows placed over the telephone were popular precautions against eavesdropping by bugging. Nor did one ever know what mail had been secretly opened.*

In early 1942, Hans, Alex, Willi Graf, and Christoph Probst were making plans to take action. Sophie joined them that May when she enrolled at the University of Munich. Although her brother initially disapproved of his sister taking part, she refused to be excluded. They found

The White Rose produced leaflets that challenged Germans to stand up to Hitler's government. Above is the second pamphlet they produced.

an ally in Professor Kurt Huber, who helped them refine their writing and took part in their discussions. The group decided to produce leaflets bearing philosophical quotes, condemnation of Hitler and Nazi policies, and calls for the German people to stand up to the threat of fascism. They did not advocate a violent revolution. Instead, they hoped to make people more aware of the wrongs being done by the government and spread discontent.

In June 1942, the first leaflet was distributed around the University of Munich. The group did so by putting them in mailboxes and leaving them to be found around campus. Others were sent through the mail, and hundreds are believed to have made it into the hands of the Gestapo. The authorities very likely immediately recognized the threat the White Rose, a name they put on the leaflets, posed.

THE FIRST LEAFLET

The first leaflet was a call for the citizens of
Germany to question the rise of the Nazis:

Nothing is so unworthy of a civilized nation as allowing itself to be governed without opposition by an irresponsible clique that has yielded to base instinct. It is certain that today every honest German is ashamed of his government. Who among us has any conception of the dimensions of shame that will befall us and our children when one day the veil has fallen from our eyes and the most horrible of crimes—crimes that infinitely outdistance every human measure—reach the light of day?

If the German people are already so corrupted and spiritually crushed that they do not raise a hand, frivolously trusting in a questionable faith in lawful order of history; if they surrender man's highest principle, that which raises him above all other God's creatures, his free will; if they abandon the will to take decisive action and turn the wheel of history and thus subject it to their own rational decision; if they are so devoid of all individuality, have already gone so far along the road toward turning into a spiritless and cowardly mass—then, yes, they deserve their downfall. Goethe speaks of the Germans as a tragic people, like the Jews and the Greeks, but today it would appear rather that they are a spineless, will-less herd of hangers-on, who now—the marrow sucked out of their bones, robbed of their center of stability—are waiting to be hounded to their destruction.[1]

So it seems—but it is not so. Rather, by means of gradual, treacherous, systematic abuse, the system has put every man into a spiritual prison. Only now, finding himself lying in fetters, has he become aware of his fate. Only a few recognized the threat of ruin, and the reward for their heroic warning was death. We will have more to say about the fate of these persons. If everyone waits until the other man makes a start, the messengers of avenging Nemesis will come steadily closer; then even the last victim will have been cast senselessly into the maw of the insatiable demon. Therefore every individual, conscious of his responsibility as a member of Christian and Western civilization, must defend himself as best he can at this late hour, he must work against the scourges of mankind, against fascism and any similar system of totalitarianism.

Offer passive resistance—resistance—wherever you may be, forestall the spread of this atheistic war machine before it is too late, before the last cities, like Cologne, have been reduced to rubble, and before the nation's last young man has given his blood on some battlefield for the hubris of a sub-human.[2] Do not forget that every people deserves the regime it is willing to endure!

From Friedrich Schiller's *The Lawgiving of Lycurgus and Solon*:[3]

"Viewed in relation to its purposes, the law code of Lycurgus is a masterpiece of political science and knowledge of human nature. He desired a powerful, unassailable state, firmly established on its own principles.

Political effectiveness and permanence were the goal toward which he strove, and he attained this goal to the full extent possible under the circumstances.

"But if one compares the purpose Lycurgus had in view with the purposes of mankind, then a deep abhorrence takes the place of the approbation which we felt at first glance. Anything may be sacrificed to the good of the state except that end for which the State serves as a means. The state is never an end in itself; it is important only as a condition under which the purpose of mankind can be attained, and this purpose is none other than the development of all man's power, his progress and improvement.

"If a state prevents the development of the capacities which reside in man, if it interferes with the progress of the human spirit, then it is reprehensible and injurious, no matter how excellently devised, how perfect in its own way. Its very permanence in that case amounts more to a reproach than to a basis for fame; it becomes a prolonged evil, and the longer it endures, the more harmful it is ...

"At the price of all moral feeling a political system was set up, and the resources of the state were mobilized to that end. In Sparta there was no conjugal love, no mother love, no filial devotion, no friendship; all men were citizens only, and all virtue was civic virtue.

"A law of the state made it the duty of Spartans to be inhumane to their slaves; in these unhappy victims of war humanity itself was insulted and mistreated. In the Spartan code of law the dangerous principle was promulgated that men are to be looked upon as means and not as ends—and the foundation of natural law and of morality were destroyed by that law ...

"What an admirable sight is afforded, by contrast, by the rough soldier Gaius Marcius in his camp before Rome, when he renounced vengeance and victory because he could not endure to see a mother's tears! ...

"The state [of Lycurgus] could endure only under the one condition: that the spirit of the people remained quiescent. Hence it could be maintained only if it failed to achieve the highest, the sole purpose of a state."

From Goethe's *The Awakening of Epimenides*, Act II, Scene 4.

SPIRITS:
Though he who has boldly risen from the abyss
Through an iron will and cunning
May conquer half the world,
Yet to the abyss he must return.
Already a terrible fear has seized him;
In vain he will resist!
And all who still stand with him
Must perish in his fall.

HOPE:
Now I find my good men
Are gathered in the night,
To wait in silence, not to sleep.
And the glorious word of liberty

They whisper and murmur,

Till in unaccustomed strangeness,

On the steps of our temple

Once again in delight they cry:

Freedom! Freedom!

Please make as many copies of this leaflet as you can and distribute them. (Feuer, 2007)

Notes:

1. Johann Wolfgang von Goethe (1749–1832) is widely considered the most important German author. He wrote poetry, plays, and prose during his long career. One of his plays is quoted at the end of the pamphlet.

2. Cologne is an important city in western Germany. Cologne was reduced to rubble by an Allied bombing raid on May 30, 1942. More than four hundred civilians died in the raid, and forty-five thousand were left homeless. By the end of the war and Allied bombings, Cologne's population was just 5 percent of its prewar number.

3. Friedrich Schiller (1759–1805) was a famous German author. His *Lawgivings of Lycurgus and Solon* contrasts two different ancient legal systems. One is that of Lycurgus, the legendary law-giver and king of Sparta who was responsible for its transformation into a state focused on war. The other is that of Solon, the Athenian ruler whose law code was considered more just and humane.

Over the course of three weeks, the group distributed more pamphlets, each offering pointed accusations and calls for resistance.

THE SECOND LEAFLET

*The second leaflet was distributed later the same month
as the first, and it contained a powerful denunciation of
Hitler's program of genocide, with an equally powerful
call for Germany to reject this behavior. The leaflet echoed
some of the concern the Scholls and Schmorell had expressed
previously—namely that this was a moment in history when
protesting was critical, or else they would have to tell future
generations that they did nothing in the face of evil. It read:*

It is impossible to engage in intellectual discourse with
National Socialist Philosophy, for if there were such an
entity, one would have to try by means of analysis and
discussion either to prove its validity or to combat it.
In actuality, however, we face a totally different situation.
At its very inception this movement depended on the
deception and betrayal of one's fellow man; even at that
time it was inwardly corrupt and could support itself only
by constant lies.

After all, Hitler states in an early edition of "his" book (a
book written in the worst German I have ever read, in
spite of the fact that it has been elevated to the position
of the Bible in this nation of poets and thinkers): "It is
unbelievable, to what extent one must betray a people in
order to rule it."[1] If at the start this cancerous growth in the
nation was not particularly noticeable, it was only because
there were still enough forces at work that operated for the
good, so that it was kept under control.

As it grew larger, however, and finally in an ultimate spurt of growth attained ruling power, the tumor broke open, as it were, and infected the whole body. The greater part of its former opponents went into hiding. The German intellectuals fled to their cellars, there, like plants struggling in the dark, away from light and sun, gradually to choke to death. Now the end is at hand. Now it is our task to find one another again, to spread information from person to person, to keep a steady purpose, and to allow ourselves no rest until the last man is persuaded of the urgent need of his struggle against this system. When thus a wave of unrest goes through the land, when "it is in the air," when many join the cause, then in a great final effort this system can be shaken off. After all, an end in terror is preferable to terror without end.

We are not in a position to draw up a final judgment about the meaning of our history. But if this catastrophe can be used to further the public welfare, it will be only by virtue of the fact that we are cleansed by suffering; that we yearn for the light in the midst of deepest night, summon our strength, and finally help in shaking off the yoke which weighs on our world.

We do not want to discuss here the question of the Jews, nor do we want in this leaflet to compose a defense or apology.[2] No, only by way of example do we want to cite the fact that since the conquest of Poland three hundred thousand Jews have been murdered in this country in the most bestial way. Here we see the most frightful crime against human dignity, a crime that is unparalleled in

the whole of history. For Jews, too, are human beings—
no matter what position we take with respect to the
Jewish question—and a crime of this dimension has been
perpetrated against human beings. Someone may say
that the Jews deserve their fate. This assertion would be a
monstrous impertinence; but let us assume that someone
said this—what position has he then taken toward the
fact that the entire Polish aristocratic youth is being
annihilated?[3] (May God grant that this program has not
yet fully achieved its aim as yet!) All male offspring of the
houses of the nobility between the ages of fifteen and twenty
were transported to concentration camps in Germany and
sentenced to forced labor, and all the girls of this age group
were sent to Norway, into the bordellos of the SS!

Why tell you these things, since you are fully aware of
them—or if not of these, then of other equally grave crimes
committed by this frightful sub-humanity? Because here
we touch on a problem which involves us deeply and forces
us all to take thought. Why do German people behave so
apathetically in the face of all these abominable crimes,
crimes so unworthy of the human race? Hardly anyone
thinks about that. It is accepted as fact and put out of mind.
The German people slumber on in their dull, stupid sleep
and encourage these fascist criminals; they give them the
opportunity to carry on their depredations; and of course
they do so. Is this a sign that the Germans are brutalized in
their simplest human feelings, that no chord within them
cries out at the sight of such deeds, that they have sunk
into a fatal consciencelessness from which they will never,

never awake? It seems to be so, and will certainly be so, if the German does not at last start up out of his stupor, if he does not protest wherever and whenever he can against this clique of criminals, if he shows no sympathy for these hundreds of thousands of victims. He must evidence not only sympathy; no, much more: a sense of complicity in guilt.

For through his apathetic behavior he gives these evil men the opportunity to act as they do; he tolerates this "government" which has taken upon itself such an infinitely great burden of guilt; indeed, he himself is to blame for the fact that it came about at all! Each man wants to be exonerated of a guilt of this kind, each one continues on his way with the most placid, the calmest conscience. But he cannot be exonerated; he is guilty, guilty, guilty! It is not too late, however, to do away with this most reprehensible of all miscarriages of government, so as to avoid being burdened with even greater guilt. Now, when in recent years our eyes have been opened, when we know exactly who our adversary is, it is high time to root out this brown horde. Up until the outbreak of the war the larger part of the German people was blinded; the Nazis did not show themselves in their true aspect. But now, now that we have recognized them for what they are, it must be the sole and first duty, the holiest duty of every German to destroy these beasts.

"If the people are barely aware that the government exists, they are happy. When the government is felt to be oppressive they are broken.

"Good fortune, alas! builds itself upon misery. Good fortune, alas! is the mask of misery. What will come of this? We cannot foresee the end. Order is upset and turns to disorder, good becomes evil. The people are confused. Is it not so, day in, day out, from the beginning?

"The wise man is therefore angular, though he does not injure others; he has sharp corners, though he does not harm; he is upright but not gruff. He is clear minded, but he does not try to be brilliant."

—Lao Tzu[4]

"Whoever undertakes to rule the kingdom and to shape it according to his whim—I foresee that he will fail to reach his goal. That is all.

"The kingdom is a living being. It cannot be constructed, in truth! He who tries to manipulate it will spoil it, he who tries to put it under his power will lose it.

"Therefore: Some creatures go out in front, others follow, some have warm breath, others cold, some are strong, some weak, some attain abundance, others succumb.

"The wise man will accordingly forswear excess, he will avoid arrogance and not overreach."

—Lao Tzu

Please make as many copies as possible of this leaflet and distribute them. (Feuer, 2007)

Notes:

1. "His" book is *Mein Kampf* ("My Struggle"), Hitler's autobiography and political work published before his rise to power.

2. The Jewish Question was the European political debate of the time over how to treat the Jewish population—who were seen as a political problem. Some argued they should be assimilated to German society or resettled in Africa or Asia. In the end, Hitler's Final Solution to the question was their mass murder.

3. As part of their effort to "Germanize" conquered territory, it is estimated that the Nazis killed close to two million non-Jewish Poles over the course of World War II. Poles, like Jews, were considered racially inferior in Nazi ideology.

4. Lao Tzu was an ancient Chinese philosopher. Although it is unlikely he was a historical person, his works are often dated to the sixth century BCE.

Hans Scholl (*right*) and Alex Schmorell (*left*) had both been in France with the German army, and there their rejection of Nazi policy solidified.

THE THIRD LEAFLET

The third leaflet, distributed in July of 1942,
was similar in theme and tone:

Salus publica suprema lex[1]

All ideal forms of government are utopias. A state cannot
be constructed on a purely theoretical basis; rather, it
must grow and ripen in the way an individual human
being matures. But we must not forget that at the starting
point of every civilization the state was already there in
rudimentary form. The family is as old as man himself,
and out of this initial bond man, endowed with reason,
created for himself a state founded on justice, whose highest
law was the common good. The state should exist as a
parallel to the divine order, and the highest of all utopias,
the *civitas dei*, is the model which in the end it should
approximate.[2] Here we will not pass judgment on the many
possible forms of the state—democracy, constitutional
monarchy, and so on.

But one matter needs to be brought out clearly and
unambiguously. Every individual human being has a
claim to a useful and just state, a state which secures
freedom of the individual as well as the good of the whole.
For, according to God's will, man is intended to pursue his
natural goal, his earthly happiness, in self-reliance and
self-chosen activity, freely and independently within the
community of life and work of the nation.

But our present "state" is the dictatorship of evil. "Oh, we've known that for a long time," I hear you object, "and it isn't necessary to bring that to our attention again." But, I ask you, if you know that, why do you not bestir yourselves, why do you allow these men who are in power to rob you step by step, openly and in secret, of one domain of your rights after another, until one day nothing, nothing at all will be left but a mechanized state system presided over by criminals and drunks? Is your spirit already so crushed by abuse that you forget it is your right—or rather, your moral duty—to eliminate this system? But if a man no longer can summon the strength to demand his right, then it is absolutely certain that he will perish. We would deserve to be dispersed through the earth like dust before the wind if we do not muster our powers at this late hour and finally find the courage which up to now we have lacked. Do not hide your cowardice behind a cloak of expediency, for with every new day that you hesitate, failing to oppose this offspring of Hell, your guilt, as in a parabolic curve, grows higher and higher.

Many, perhaps most, of the readers of these leaflets do not see clearly how they can practice an effective opposition. They do not see any avenues open to them. We want to try to show them that everyone is in a position to contribute to the overthrow of this system. It is not possible through solitary withdrawal, in the manner of embittered hermits, to prepare the ground for the overturn of this "government" or bring about the revolution at the earliest possible moment. No, it can be done only by the cooperation of many convinced, energetic people—people who are agreed as to the means they must use to attain their goal. We have no great number of choices as to these means. The only one available is passive resistance.

The meaning and the goal of passive resistance is to topple National Socialism, and in this struggle we must not recoil from any course, any action, whatever its nature. At all points we must oppose National Socialism, wherever it is open to attack. We must soon bring this monster of a state to an end. A victory of fascist Germany in this war would have immeasurable, frightful consequences. The military victory over Bolshevism dare not become the primary concern of the Germans.[3] The defeat of the Nazis must unconditionally be the first order of business, the greater necessity of this latter requirement will be discussed in one of our forthcoming leaflets.

And now every convinced opponent of National Socialism must ask himself how he can fight against the present "state" in the most effective way, how he can strike it the most telling blows. Through passive resistance, without a doubt. We cannot provide each man with the blueprint for his acts, we can only suggest them in general terms, and he alone will find the way of achieving this end:

Sabotage in armament plants and war industries, sabotage at all gatherings, rallies, public ceremonies, and organizations of the National Socialist Party. Obstruction of the smooth functioning of the war machine (a machine for war that goes on solely to shore up and perpetuate the

National Socialist Party and its dictatorship). Sabotage in all the areas of science and scholarship which further the continuation of the war—whether in universities, technical schools, laboratories, research institutes, or technical bureaus. Sabotage in all cultural institutions which could potentially enhance the "prestige" of the fascists among the people. Sabotage in all branches of the arts which have even the slightest dependence on National Socialism or render it service.

Sabotage in all publications, all newspapers, that are in the pay of the "government" and that defend its ideology and aid in disseminating the brown lie. Do not give a penny to public drives (even when they are conducted under the pretense of charity). For this is only a disguise. In reality the proceeds aid neither the Red Cross nor the needy. The government does not need this money; it is not financially interested in these money drives. After all, the presses run continuously to manufacture any desired amount of paper currency. But the populace must be kept constantly under tension, the pressure of the bit must not be allowed to slacken! Do not contribute to the collections of metal, textiles, and the like. Try to convince all your acquaintances, including those in the lower social classes, of the senselessness of continuing, of the hopelessness of this war; of our spiritual and economic enslavement at the hands of the National Socialists; of the destruction of all moral and religious values; and urge them to passive resistance!

Aristotle, *Politics*:[4] "And further, it is part [of the nature of tyranny] to strive to see to it that nothing is kept hidden of that which any subject says or does, but that everywhere he will be spied upon, ... and further, to set man against the privileged and the wealthy. Also it is part of these tyrannical measures, to keep the subjects poor, in order to pay the guards and soldiers, and so that they will be occupied with earning their livelihood and will have neither leisure nor opportunity to engage in conspiratorial acts ... Further, [to levy] such taxes on income as were imposed in Syracuse, for under Dionysius the citizens gladly paid out their whole fortunes in taxes within five years. Also, the tyrant is inclined constantly to ferment wars."[5]

Please duplicate and distribute! (Feuer, 2007)

Notes:

1. A Latin phrase that means "the good of the people should be the highest law."

2. A Latin phrase that means "the city of God." Here, it refers to an idealized heavenly utopia.

3. "Bolshevism" was often used as a synonym for "Communism" at the time the pamphlet was written.

4. Aristotle (384–322 BCE) was an ancient Greek philosopher. His work *Politics* is an influential work of political philosophy.

5. Syracuse was an ancient Greek city located in modern-day Italy, and Dionysius was a historical leader of Syracuse.

THE FOURTH LEAFLET

After their initial rapid flurry of publication, the group
paused in late 1942. They resumed their activity in
early 1943, producing their fourth leaflet:

There is an ancient maxim that we repeat to our children:
"He who won't listen will have to feel." But a wise child will
not burn his fingers the second time on a hot stove. In the
past weeks Hitler has choked up successes in Africa and
in Russia. In consequence, optimism on the one hand and
distress and pessimism on the other have grown within
the German people with a rapidity quite inconsistent with
traditional German apathy. On all sides one hears among
Hitler's opponents—the better segments of the population—
exclamations of despair, words of disappointment and
discouragement, often ending with the question: "Will Hitler
now, after all ...?"

Meanwhile, the German offensive against Egypt has ground
to a halt. Rommel has to bide his time in a dangerously
exposed position.[1] But the push into the East proceeds. This
apparent success has been purchased at the most horrible
expense of human life, and so it can no longer be counted an
advantage. Therefore we must warn against all optimism.

Neither Hitler nor Goebbels can have counted the dead.[2] In
Russia thousands are lost daily. It is the time of the harvest,
and the reaper cuts into the ripe grain with wide strokes.
Mourning takes up her abode in the country cottages,
and there is no one to dry the tears of the mothers.

Yet Hitler feeds with lies those people whose most precious belongings he has stolen and whom he has driven to a meaningless death.

Every word that comes from Hitler's mouth is a lie. When he says peace, he means war, and when he blasphemously uses the name of the Almighty, he means the power of evil, the fallen angel, Satan. His mouth is the foul-smelling maw of Hell, and his might is at bottom accursed. True, we must conduct a struggle against the National Socialist terrorist state with rational means; but whoever today still doubts the reality, the existence of demonic powers, has failed by a wide margin to understand the metaphysical background of this war. Behind the concrete, the visible events, behind all objective, logical considerations, we find the irrational element: The struggle against the demon, against the servants of the Antichrist.

Everywhere and at all times demons have been lurking in the dark, waiting for the moment when man is weak; when of his own volition he leaves his place in the order of Creation as founded for him by God in freedom; when he yields to the force of evil, separates himself from the powers of a higher order; and after voluntarily taking the first step, he is driven on to the next and the next at a furiously accelerating rate. Everywhere and at all times of greatest trial men have appeared, prophets and saints who cherished their freedom, who preached the One God and who His help brought the people to a reversal of their downward course. Man is free, to be sure, but without the true God he is defenseless against the principle of evil. He is like a rudderless ship, at the mercy of the storm, an infant without his mother, a cloud dissolving into thin air.

I ask you, you as a Christian wrestling for the preservation of your greatest treasure, whether you hesitate, whether you incline toward intrigue, calculation, or procrastination in the hope that someone else will raise his arm in your defense? Has God not given you the strength, the will to fight? We must attack evil where it is strongest, and it is strongest in the power of Hitler.

"So I returned, and considered all the oppressions that are done under the sun: and behold the tears of such as were oppressed, and they had no comforter; and on the side of their oppressors there was power; but they had no comforter. Wherefore I praised the dead which are already dead than the living which are yet alive."

—Ecclesiastes 4[3]

"True anarchy is the generative element of religion. Out of the annihilation of every positive element she lifts her gloriously radiant countenance as the founder of a new world ... If Europe were about to awaken again, if a state of states, a teaching of political science were at hand! Should hierarchy then ... be the principle of the union of states? Blood will stream over Europe until the nations become aware of the frightful madness which drives them in circles. And then, struck by celestial music and made gentle, they approach their former altars all together, hear about the works of peace, and hold a great celebration of peace with fervent tears before the smoking altars. Only religion can reawaken Europe, establish the rights of the peoples, and install Christianity in new splendor visibly on earth in its office as guarantor of peace."

—Novalis[4]

We wish expressly to point out that the White Rose is not in the pay of any foreign power. Though we know that National Socialist power must be broken by military means, we are trying to achieve a renewal from within of the severely wounded German spirit. This rebirth must be preceded, however, by the clear recognition of all the guilt with which the German people have burdened themselves, and by an uncompromising battle against Hitler and his all too many minions, party members, Quislings, and the like.[5] With total brutality the chasm that separates the better portion of the nation from everything that is opened wide. For Hitler and his followers there is no punishment on this Earth commensurate with their crimes.

But out of love for coming generations we must make an example after the conclusion of the war, so that no one will ever again have the slightest urge to try a similar action. And do not forget the petty scoundrels in this regime; note their names, so that none will go free! They should not find it possible, having had their part in these abominable crimes, at the last minute to rally to another flag and then act as if nothing had happened! To set you at rest, we add that the addresses of the readers of the White Rose are not recorded in writing. They were picked at random from directories.

We will not be silent. We are your bad conscience. The White Rose will not leave you in peace! (Feuer, 2007)

Notes:

1. Edwin Rommel was the famous general who commanded German forces in North Africa at the time.
2. Joseph Goebbels was a high-ranking official of Nazi Germany and close confidante of Hitler.
3. Ecclesiastes is a book in the Old Testament of the Bible.
4. Novalis, the penname of Friedrich Leopold, Baron von Hardenberg (1772–1801), was a German mystic and philosopher.
5. "Quisling" means traitor. The word derives from the Nazi collaborator Vidkun Quisling, who led the Norwegian government under German occupation.

THE FIFTH LEAFLET

Their fifth leaflet, called A Call to All Germans, *came in January as well, after the defeat of Germany at Stalingrad. This particular leaflet caused concern in the government, with an investigation launched by the Gestapo. It read in part:*

Germans! Do you and your children want to suffer the same fate that befell the Jews? Do you want to be judged by the same standards as your traducers?[1] Are we to be forever a nation which is hated and rejected by all mankind? No. Dissociate yourselves from National Socialist gangsters. Prove by your deeds that you think otherwise. A new war of liberation is about to begin. The better part of the nation will fight on our side. Cast off the cloak of indifference you have wrapped around you. Make the decision before it is too late.

Do not believe the National Socialist propaganda which has driven the fear of Bolshevism into your bones.

Do not believe that Germany's welfare is linked to the victory of National Socialism for good or ill. A criminal regime cannot achieve a German victory. Separate yourselves in time from everything connected with National Socialism. In the aftermath a terrible but just judgment will be meted out to those who stayed in hiding, who were cowardly and hesitant.

What can we learn from the outcome of this war—this war that never was a national war?

The imperialist ideology of force, from whatever side it comes, must be shattered for all time. A one-sided Prussian militarism must never again be allowed to assume power.[2] Only in large-scale cooperation among the nations of Europe can the ground be prepared for reconstruction. Centralized hegemony, such as the Prussian state has tried to exercise in Germany and in Europe, must be cut down at its inception.[3] The Germany of the future must be a federal state. At this juncture only a sound federal system can imbue a weakened Europe with a new life. The workers must be liberated from their condition of down trodden slavery under National Socialism. The illusory structure of autonomous national industry must disappear. Every nation and each man have a right to the goods of the whole world!

Freedom of speech, freedom of religion, the protection of individual citizens from the arbitrary will of criminal regimes of violence—these will be the bases of the New Europe.

Support the resistance. Distribute the leaflets! (Feuer, 2007)

Notes:
1. "Traducer" means slanderer.
2. Here "Prussian" refers to the Prussian people from North Germany, who unified Germany and were renowned for their militarism and willingness to follow orders.
3. "Hegemony" means dominance or being the most powerful.

In mid-January 1943, Paul Giesler, a Nazi Party leader in Bavaria, spoke at the University of Munich and made clear that the government was keeping an eye on the students. Speaking out against the "twisted Intellects" the university was seemingly producing, he told the audience that "real life is transmitted to us only by Adolf Hitler." He also attacked women in the audience, who he felt should be with their families. A riot broke out following his remarks. It was an aggressive speech that was intended to send a message: we know you're here. But the White Rose wasn't afraid and prepared their next pamphlet.

THE SIXTH LEAFLET
AND ITS CONSEQUENCES

On February 18, 1943, Sophie and Hans Scholl took hundreds of their latest leaflet, now known as Fellow Fighters in the Resistance, *to the University of Munich. The leaflet read:*

Fellow Fighters in the Resistance!

Shaken and broken, our people behold the loss of the men of Stalingrad.[1] Three hundred and thirty thousand German men have been senselessly and irresponsibly driven to death and destruction by the inspired strategy of our World War I Private First Class.[2] Führer, we thank you!

The German people are in ferment. Will we continue to entrust the fate of our armies to a dilettante? Do we want to sacrifice the rest of German youth to the base ambitions of a Party clique? No, never! The day of reckoning has come—the reckoning of German youth with the most abominable tyrant our people have ever been forced to endure. In the name of German youth we demand restitution by Adolf Hitler's state of our personal freedom, the most precious treasure we have, out of which he has swindled us in the most miserable way.

We grew up in a state in which all free expression of opinion is unscrupulously suppressed. The Hitler Youth, the SA, the SS have tried to drug us, to revolutionize us, to regiment us in the most promising young years of our lives. "Philosophical training" is the name given to the despicable method by which our budding intellectual development is muffled in a fog of empty phrases. A system of selection of leaders at once unimaginably devilish and narrow-minded trains up its future party bigwigs in the "Castles of the Knightly Order" to become Godless, impudent, and conscienceless exploiters and executioners—blind, stupid hangers-on of the Führer. We "Intellectual Workers" are the ones who should put obstacles in the path of this caste of overlords.

Soldiers at the front are regimented like schoolboys by student leaders and trainees for the post of Gauleiter, and the lewd jokes of the Gauleiters insult the honor of the women students.[3] German women students at the university in Munich have given a dignified reply to the besmirching of their honor, and German students have defended the women in the universities and have stood firm ... That is a beginning of the struggle for our free self-determination—without which intellectual and spiritual values cannot be created. We thank the brave comrades, both men and women, who have set us brilliant examples.

For us there is but one slogan: fight against the party! Get out of the party organization, which are used to keep our mouths sealed and hold us in political bondage! Get out of the lecture rooms of the SS corporals and sergeants and the party bootlickers! We want genuine learning and real freedom of opinion. No threat can terrorize us, not even the shutting down of the institutions of higher learning. This is the struggle of each and every one of us for our future, our freedom, and our honor under a regime conscious of its moral responsibility.

Freedom and honor! For ten long years Hitler and his coadjutor have manhandled, squeezed, twisted, and debased these two splendid German words to the point of nausea, as only dilettantes can, casting the highest values of a nation before swine. They have sufficiently demonstrated in the ten years of destruction of all material and intellectual freedom, of all moral substance among the German people, what they understand by freedom and honor. The frightful bloodbath has opened the eyes of even the stupidest German—it is a slaughter which they arranged in the name of "freedom and honor of the German nation" throughout Europe, and which they daily start anew.

The name of Germany is dishonored for all time if German youth does not finally rise, take revenge, and atone, smash its tormentors, and set up a new Europe of the spirit. Students! The German people look to us. As in 1813 the people expected us to shake off the Napoleonic yoke, so in 1943 they look to us to break the National Socialist terror through the power of the spirit.[4] Beresina and Stalingrad are burning in the East.[5] The dead of Stalingrad implore us to take action. "Up, up, my people, let smoke and flame be our sign!"[6]

Our people stand ready to rebel against the National Socialist enslavement of Europe in a fervent new breakthrough of freedom and honor. (Feuer, 2007)

Notes:

1. Stalingrad is the Russian city that gave its name to the Battle of Stalingrad. The German defeat there resulted in more than eight hundred thousand German casualties and marked the turning point of the war. The German army was never again able to match Soviet forces after losing so many men.
2. "Private First Class" is a reference to Hitler's low rank during World War I.
3. A "Gauleiter" was a regional leader of the Nazi Party.

4. "Napoleonic yoke" refers to how, in 1813, the German states were under the control of Napoleonic France.

5. Beresina was the site of one of Napoleon's defeats in Russia. His failed invasion of Russia would lead to his overthrow, just as Germany's 1943 loss at Stalingrad marked the beginning of the end for Hitler.

6. A reference to a poem by Theodor Körner (1791–1813), a German poet and soldier who died in the German fight against Napoleon's rule.

After leaving stacks of the leaflet around campus to be found by students leaving lectures, they climbed some stairs that overlooked the entrance hall of the building. Sophie let a few drop from her hands to scatter across the floor below, where a building superintendent and member of the Nazi Party named Jakob Schmid saw them and alerted the Gestapo. "The doors of the building were immediately locked, and the fate of brother and sister was sealed," Inge wrote later. The Scholls were arrested on the spot, and after finding evidence with Christoph Probst's name on it at Hans's flat, he was arrested as well.

While tossing leaflets from a balcony at the University of Munich (pictured here), Hans and Sophie Scholl were caught by the Gestapo.

The White Rose Movement: Nonviolent Resistance to the Nazis

The Trial

After hours of interrogation, the Scholls and Probst were charged with treason. They confessed to their activities and took full responsibility, in hopes of sparing the rest of the White Rose. The government moved fast; the three were arrested on February 18 and went to trial on February 22, with no time for their families to see them before they went before the judge. At their trial, the three were not allowed to choose a lawyer to defend them, and they made no attempt to disprove the charges against them. When it was over, the judge sentenced them to death.

The three were executed later that day, by guillotine. They were allowed to see each other one last time before their sentence was carried out in the yard of Stadelheim Prison in Munich. Their parents were able to see them as they were brought out, and Inge remembered her brother's strength, writing that he showed no fear in the face of death. His last words before being beheaded were, "Long live freedom!" He, Sophie, and Probst are buried together near the place where they were killed.

The same day, the newspaper *Münchner Neueste Nachrichten* wrote about the trial. As all media was controlled by the Nazi Party, it showed the concern the White Rose activity had inspired in the highest echelons of government and how quickly the state wanted to control

THE RED ORCHESTRA

Most of the resistance groups working against Hitler were isolated and did not communicate or coordinate. Despite this, three groups were put under investigation by the Nazi government under the term the "Red Orchestra." Although they did not work together, all three "units" had ties to communism and the Soviet Union, and all three sought to overthrow Hitler. Multiple departments in the Nazi government, including the secret police, were assigned to gather information and watch the units that made up the group.

One was the Trepper unit, which was based in Germany as well as France and Belgium. Under the leadership of Leopold Trepper, the seven different branches of the group worked to gather intelligence on the Nazi military and their strength in Western Europe. To do so, they infiltrated the military ranks and learned about their plans, which they sent to the Soviet Union. Although Trepper was arrested in 1943, he was released in order to become a double agent. Instead, he went into hiding and joined the French Resistance.

The Schulze-Boysen/Harnack group was created by a Luftwaffe officer named Harro Schulze-Boysen, who was opposed to Hitler and used his place in the Luftwaffe and Nazi Party to spy. His network grew substantially, and in 1936 he was able to contact Arvid Harnack, who organized a resistance circle of his own. Together with the large network of people they built up, they worked to help people flee Germany and shared intelligence with the Soviet Union and the United States. They also worked

to spread awareness of Nazi crimes in a similar way to the White Rose, producing leaflets designed to inspire civil disobedience and posting anti-Nazi propaganda around cities. After the Gestapo decoded their radio transmissions in 1942, Schulze-Boysen and Harnack, along with their wives, were arrested and executed.

The third unit that made up the Red Orchestra was the Red Three, a group based in Switzerland with ties to Germany. It was started in 1936 by Alexander Rado, a Hungarian Communist. Like the others in the Red Orchestra, the Red Three were engaged in espionage across German territory and shared the information they gathered with the Soviet Union and Great Britain through the Lucy spy ring. Rado was not arrested by the German authorities but was imprisoned in the Soviet Union after the war on charges of spying for the United Kingdom and the United States.

These groups shared crucial information with the Allies despite the close attention of the Nazi authorities, and their actions underscore the widespread—if isolated—attempts to undermine Nazi power from the early 1930s through the end of the war in 1945. While the White Rose worked publically through their leaflets, the Red Orchestra worked largely in secret, pulling strings and using wide networks to gather what information they could to share with contacts outside of Germany. This work, like that of the White Rose, was extremely dangerous, and today these groups are remembered as brave examples of effective espionage.

The Scholls and Probst are buried next to each other in Munich, not far from where they were executed.

the narrative by casting the Scholls and Probst as its most classic enemies: outsiders bent on destroying the country.

In the following months, more members of the White Rose were found and tried, with some of them executed. Kurt Huber and Alexander Schmorell were executed on July 13, and Willi Graf was executed on October 12. The verdict in their trial read in part, "During a time of war, Alexander Schmorell, Kurt Huber, and Wilhelm Graf used leaflets to call for sabotage of armaments and for the overthrow of the National Socialist way of life; they have propagated defeatist thinking and vilified the Führer in a most vulgar manner, thereby aiding and abetting the enemies of the Reich and demoralizing our armed forces. They are therefore to be punished by death. They have forfeited their honor as citizens for ever."

Others, including fringe members who had provided some support, were sentenced to prison terms. Within just one year of distributing their first pamphlet, the White Rose movement came to an end.

The Allied forces dropped copies of the final White Rose leaflet over Germany.

CHAPTER FOUR

The Effects of the White Rose Movement

Measuring the effects of the White Rose movement is difficult. The group was small, and their activities took place over a short period of time. Sadly, the war and Hitler's rule continued for more than two years after the first White Rose executions took place. Their work was an example of nonviolent resistance in the face of a threat so great that it alone could not topple the regime, and they knew that. Instead, their goal was always to bring forth a better Germany through appeals to a sense of decency that seemed to have been lost in their country. Unable to take the lead in the military revolt they knew would be necessary to overthrow Hitler, they nonetheless turned to their peers and fellow residents of Munich in an attempt to make them see the truth.

Given that their goal was to rouse the German people to resistance, it would be easy to say that the White Rose was unsuccessful. But that assessment misses the ultimate importance of what the Scholls, Alexander Schmorell, Christoph Probst, and others undertook: when they saw what was happening, they stood up against it and made their voices heard at a time when few—if any—others were willing or able to do so.

The activities of the White Rose movement ended abruptly, but not completely, in 1943. That year, a copy of their final leaflet was smuggled out of Germany and given to the Allied forces, which dropped thousands of copies from planes into Germany. More recently, translations of what would have been the movement's seventh leaflet have become available. It was written largely by Christoph Probst, and reads in part:

"

> *Today Germany is as encircled as Stalingrad was. Will all Germans be sacrificed to the harbinger of hate and destruction? To him, who tortured the Jews, who eradicated half of the Poles, who desired the annihilation of Russia—to him who took away liberty, peace, happiness, hope, and joy, and gave us inflationary money instead? This*

ought not, this must not be. Hitler and his regime must fall so that Germany can live. Make your decision, Stalingrad and downfall, or Tripoli and a hopeful future. And once you have decided, act.

A Symbolic Victory

Like all members of the White Rose (except Professor Huber), Sophie and Hans Scholl were average German students. They had been part of the Hitler Youth programs that all young people took part in, and Hans had spent time with the military caring for soldiers. Had these young people not started the White Rose, it is likely we would never have heard their names. They would have been forgotten to history as among the many German citizens who got by under Hitler's government.

But instead, we know them as heroes because they decided to do something in the face of evil. They wrote and distributed six leaflets over the course of nine months between 1942 and 1943, all of which were intended not to start a revolution but to remind the German people of what was taking place so that they could not ignore it as they had been. Inspired by their deep sense of right and wrong, and the knowledge that they had a shared responsibility to make their voices heard, they did just that, as Kurt Huber said in court in February 1943:

> *What I intended to accomplish was to rouse the student body, not by means of an organization, but solely by my simple words; to urge them, not to violence, but to moral insight into the existing serious deficiencies of our political system. To urge the return to clear moral principles, to the constitutional state, to mutual trust between men.*

It took immense bravery to contradict the Nazis' propaganda and messaging. The Scholls and their allies knew what they were risking when they decided to start their activities but chose to do so anyway because they believed so strongly that they had a moral obligation to do so. George Wittenstein wrote later:

> *Producing and distributing such leaflets sounds simple from today's perspective, but, in reality, it was not only very difficult but even dangerous. Paper was scarce, as were envelopes. And if one bought them in large quantities, or for that matter, more than just a few postage stamps (in any larger numbers), one would (have) become instantly suspect. Taking leaflets to other cities carried great risk, because trains*

*were constantly patrolled by military police, who
demanded identification papers of any male of
military service age. Anyone traveling without
official marching papers was AWOL—and the
consequences predictable. Some of us traveled
in civilian clothing, hoping for the best, some
with forged travel orders, I myself used false
identification papers (my cousin's with whom
I shared a certain resemblance). We left the
briefcases which contained the leaflets in a
different compartment, for luggage was routinely
searched. Mostly, however, leaflets were taken
by female students who were not subject to
such scrutiny.*

The White Rose broke a culture of silence, which in and of itself is a symbolic victory that speaks to the ability of a few people to make a difference. While it is impossible to know how the public reacted to the White Rose activities, the fact that today they are remembered as heroes suggests that those who were living in fear in Nazi Germany might have found solace in the brave acts of these young people.

Inge Scholl later wrote that the movement was about increasing awareness and promoting nonviolent resistance. She said the group's efforts required complete anonymity to thrive and spread their message that not the entire

This commemorative stamp features Sophie Scholl.

population supported Hitler. The Scholls didn't know it at the time, but their work was part of a much larger network of resistance that took place across German territory. Spies were working behind the scenes to undermine the German war machine, while bombings and other sabotage were carried out against infrastructure. They were not alone, but in the lengths to which they went in public, they were.

Their activity also overlapped with the Battle of Stalingrad, the point at which the war turned against Germany and an understanding of possible defeat permeated German society. It inspired the White Rose's final leaflets, although the Scholls and Probst, as well as others, did not live to see the end of the war that came just over two years later.

Life After War

After the war, Germany was left in near ruin. Many cities had been bombed to near destruction during the war, and millions had died. But the country wasn't left to its own devices. Instead, at the Potsdam Conference of summer 1945, the Allied powers agreed to a framework to govern the country between them. It included provisions to encourage democratization and disarmament, as well as altering the German economy so that the removal of war-related industries would not decimate the economy. They focused efforts on building Germany's agricultural and light-industrial output, and the agreement also allowed for Germans in formerly held areas such as Poland or Hungary to be transferred back to Germany. Reparations to the Soviet Union were formalized as well.

The country was divided between the United Kingdom, the United States, and France in the West, and the Soviet Union in the East. The same divisions were also made in Berlin, where the Berlin Wall would become a symbol of the Soviet Union's restrictions on personal freedom and freedom of movement. Thanks to economic investment from Europe and the Marshall Plan, which pumped money into European countries destroyed by the war, Germany experienced significant economic growth in the decades following the war. This is true of both East and West Germany, although to a greater extent in the West than in the state-controlled economy of the East. The country would not be united again until 1990, with the Treaty of the Final Settlement with Respect to Germany, which was negotiated between the governments of East and West Germany along with France, the Soviet Union, the United Kingdom, and the United States.

The Allied powers also undertook the process of denazification, or the removal of any Nazi influence in

Germany's culture, politics, legal system, or society. It was an unpopular process overall and was eventually phased out. The United States military took over the process to start, and the military was vigorous about identifying and prosecuting those who had ties to the Nazi regime, establishing a system by which Germans who were members of the Nazi Party were ranked from Major Offenders to Followers to Exonerated Persons. Those who were involved with the Nazi Party were barred from holding public office and some careers; in 1947, 1.9 million people were only able to legally hold "manual labor" jobs. By 1946, with a backlog of millions of files to be processed, Germany took over the process and introduced regional tribunals to establish adherence to Nazi ideology and level of involvement with the party apparatus, as well as responsibility for the most heinous crimes committed by the state. They also used censorship of art and the media to ensure that anything that could be seen as pro-Nazism was not published.

The Nuremberg Trials were held for about a year between November 1945 and October 1946. These would become some of the most influential trials in international law, with twenty-two of the most high ranking Nazi officials facing charges on war crimes and crimes against humanity. It also gave the world its first look at the bureaucracy behind the horror that was the Nazi regime and the Holocaust. The hearings were presided over by judges from the Allied countries and took place at the International Military Tribunal. During the course of the trial, evidence about human rights abuses was shown, including witness statements and video of what was found at concentration and death camps when Allied forces liberated them.

Based on the findings of the Nuremberg Trials, the International Criminal Court was established to ensure that those who commit crimes against humanity can be held accountable. The Geneva Conventions, signed in 1949, were also the result of the Holocaust. These treaties established norms during warfare, including treatment of prisoners of war. Today, the Geneva Conventions are the primary governing documents that bind states—although atrocities, including genocide, have taken place since.

Collective Guilt

Shortly after the war, the moral question the Scholls had anticipated started being asked. How could the German people let the Holocaust happen, and what was their responsibility in its aftermath? Questions about what was known by whom have long plagued our understanding of the human rights abuses and war crimes that took place during Hitler's reign, but it is clear that the average German was aware that programs targeting Jews and other minorities were underway in the 1930s.

The Allies felt it was important that the German people grapple with their role in the atrocities Hitler carried out. In 1945, Britain green-lit broadcasts and newspaper features that put some of the responsibility on the German people, and US forces believed that being aware of collective guilt was necessary for the German state to move forward politically. Collective guilt did not mean that all Germans shared equal responsibility. Instead, it underlined the role of bystanders in allowing crimes against humanity to take place. Although Hitler and his inner circle bore most of the blame, average citizens who accepted these actions had to confront what took place on their watch. It was exactly what the Scholls had considered when they asked what, when the war ended, they could say they did to stop it.

Germans were forced to confront what took place during the Holocaust almost immediately. German prisoners of war were shown films of what was found at concentration camps. Civilians and soldiers alike were tasked with transporting bodies to graves or were brought to camps to see firsthand the large number of victims. The Allies also produced posters with images from the camps emblazoned with messages like, "These Atrocities: Your Fault!"

The question of collective German guilt has long been controversial, with some favoring the term "collective responsibility" or rejecting the idea that the group is responsible for the actions of the few. For this reason, the role of the average German citizen in the atrocities of the Nazi regime remains a puzzle for the international community. Numerous books, articles, and films have been made on the subject, and the question of how the atrocities fit into German identity is heavily debated. In some ways, the global community struggles with the legacy of the Holocaust as well. In the United States, the rejection of Jewish refugees in the years before the Holocaust is seen as a reminder of the world's role in ensuring the safety of vulnerable populations. Additionally, the memory of the Holocaust is recalled often when talking about crimes against humanity in countries like the Central African Republic and Syria.

The sheer scale of the Holocaust and the repression of the Nazi regime may be difficult for humanity to comprehend for centuries to come. But the very concept of collective guilt seems to underline what the White Rose stood for: that everyone, no matter what their role, had a responsibility to try to stop Hitler—and those who did not use any means available to them to stand in his way must grapple with their moral choices.

Legacy of Bravery

Today, the White Rose is one of the most famous of the Nazi-era resistance movements, and it is an important example of student-led nonviolent resistance. Monuments to their bravery stand around Germany, including on the

Films like *Sophie Scholl: The Final Days* have been made to honor the legacy and impact of the White Rose.

University of Munich campus, where they spread their leaflets and were ultimately captured by the Gestapo. Alexander Schmorell, who worshipped in the Russian Orthodox Church, was made a saint in 2012 in recognition of his work with the White Rose.

Films have been made about them and books have been written, and today on social media people mark the anniversary of their execution by sharing their work and photos. Lillian Garrett-Groag, who wrote a play about the group titled *The White Rose*, told *Newsday* in 1993, "It is possibly the most spectacular moment of resistance that I can think of in the twentieth century … The fact that five little kids, in the mouth of the wolf, where it really

The White Rose Movement: Nonviolent Resistance to the Nazis

counted, had the tremendous courage to do what they did, is spectacular to me. I know that the world is better for them having been there, but I don't know why."

The White Rose movement was one of the first student-led organizations to challenge those in power, and it was far from the last. In fact, across the world, university students have sparked change and started conversations through nonviolent resistance for generations. In Latin America, university students were at the vanguard of challenging repressive governments and international interference in state affairs during the 1970s and 1980s. In 1968, countries from France to Pakistan saw a wave of student-led protests challenging dictatorship, educational policies, and emergency rule. In 1978, students in Iran were among the first to begin protests that would topple the monarchy the next year, bringing about the Islamic Revolution; in 2009 they marched again, this time to protest election results seen as fraudulent. In 2011, students were at the forefront of the Arab Spring movements that swept through the Middle East, toppling dictatorships in Libya, Tunisia, and Egypt. In the United States, college campuses have been the scene of protests from the Great Depression of 1929 to the Great Recession of 2008. Almost every country around the world has a history of student activism—and that is a history into which the White Rose falls.

What the White Rose has come to mean to Germany is significant. Their story has helped others who lived at that time fully understand what took place and what their role was; Hitler's own personal secretary, Traudl Junge, wrote in her autobiography:

> One day I went past the memorial plaque which had been put up for Sophie Scholl ... I saw that she was born the same year as me, and she was executed the same year I started working for Hitler. And at that moment I actually sensed that it was no excuse to be young, and that it would have been possible to find things out.

As Germany and the world continues to work through how Hitler came to power and what responsibility the country must morally bear, the White Rose stands for a better Germany. "They permit us to believe that at the time not all Germans were mute and cowardly followers," German president Joachim Gauck has said about the movement.

Around the world, the White Rose has also served as inspiration for programs ranging from Holocaust remembrance to genocide prevention. The closing words of the fourth leaflet, "We will not be silent," were used as a slogan during protests against the 2003 Iraq War. Although not in the spirit of the White Rose movement, antiwar protesters have used their name on hoax bombs,

THE WHITE ROSE MOVEMENT REMEMBERED

Since the 1970s, the White Rose movement has been the basis for films, TV specials, books, and even operas. The earliest were three films; *The Promise* was made in 1970, while *The Last Five Days* and *The White Rose* were made in 1982. In 1986, Udo Zimmerman composed an opera about the group, called *White Rose*, which premiered in Hamburg before touring internationally. It has just two roles, those of Hans and Sophie, and tells the story of their activism and eventual death.

In 1991, Lillian Garrett-Groag's play, also called *The White Rose*, premiered at the Old Globe Theater. It focuses on the latter days of the Scholls. Garrett-Groag ends the play with Robert Mohr, head of the Gestapo, remarking, "The most we can hope for is to get by," a line intended to highlight the bravery of the Scholls and the role of choice in confronting or allowing atrocities to take place.

In 2005, Marc Rothemund and Fred Breinersdorfer made a film about Sophie Scholl, titled *Sophie Scholl: The Final Days*. The film follows Sophie and Hans as they are captured by the Gestapo, interrogated, put on trial, and executed. The film gave Sophie the last words, "The sun is still shining," which are not believed to be her true final words. Sophie is played by Julia Jentsch, who was awarded Best Actress honors at the Berlin Film Festival, European Film Awards, and the German Film Awards in 2005. The film was nominated for but did not win the Best Foreign Language Film Oscar at the Academy Awards.

A statue of Sophie Scholl in a hall of fame in southern Germany

including five that were placed around US military recruitment centers in 2007 and 2008.

In 2003, a German competition was held to name the greatest Germans of all time. Among those surveyed under the age of forty, Hans and Sophie Scholl were voted fourth, landing ahead of Johann Sebastian Bach and Albert Einstein. This highlights the continued importance and appreciation for the Scholls and the White Rose movement, as generations who never knew the horrors of Nazi Germany can see the bravery and strength these young people showed.

The White Rose movement was a group of fewer than ten friends and a professor they trusted who spoke truth to power in a moment in history when it was nearly unheard of. With just six leaflets and a willingness to confront the sacrifice they were forced to make, they rattled the establishment of Nazi Germany to its core and showed that dissent was a matter of patriotism and compassion. Today, we remember them because they stood strong in the face of tyranny, while not engaging in violence themselves. Although they were killed in their early twenties, their memory and courage live on.

CHRONOLOGY

1919   The Treaty of Versailles is signed.

1920   Adolf Hitler joins German Workers' Party, which becomes the Nazi Party.

1923   The Beer Hall Putsch takes place; Hitler is arrested.

1925   The Nazi Party is founded again, following Hitler's release from prison.

1929   Stock market crash triggers a global economic depression.

1933   After rapid growth in support, Hitler is named chancellor of Germany. The Enabling Act is also passed, giving Hitler extreme power.

1934   Night of the Long Knives purges Hitler's possible rivals.

1938   Kristallnacht escalates the persecution of Jews in Germany.

1939   World War II begins with invasion of Poland.

1942   White Rose movement founded at the University of Munich; the first four leaflets are distributed.

1943   Battle of Stalingrad leaves German forces in retreat. The Scholls and Christoph Probst caught by Gestapo; they are executed the same day as their trial. The White Rose movement is broken up by arrests, executions, and imprisonment.

1945   Hitler dies by suicide; World War II ends.

GLOSSARY

anti-Semitism Bigotry and prejudice against Jews.

Beer Hall Putsch An attempted revolt led by Hitler in 1923.

chancellor The appointed leader of Germany; after the war, it became an elected position.

genocide Deliberate and targeted mass killing of a particular ethnic, religious, or other minority group.

German Workers' Party An early nationalist party that eventually because the Nazi Party.

Gestapo Adolf Hitler's secret police.

hyperinflation Rapid and uncontrolled increase in costs; hyperinflation is generally acknowledged when prices rise more than 50 percent in a single month.

Mein Kampf Hitler's memoir and manifesto that was completed during his 1924 prison term. It outlines his beliefs and vision for Germany.

nationalism Intense patriotism to one's country over all else that is often characterized by superiority.

National Socialist German Workers' Party The full name of the Nazi Party.

Nazi Germany A term used for the country of Germany under Hitler's rule from 1933 to 1945.

nonviolent resistance A form of protest that does not use violence. Nonviolent resistance can include protest, hunger strikes, or other means of registering disapproval.

paramilitary An unofficial military force that is often tied to a political party or group.

populism A political style that appeals to a wide portion of society either through policies that directly appeal to average voters or through a style that wins support.

Reichstag The German parliament building.

Roma European nomadic minority.

SA *Sturmabteilung*, or "Storm Detachment." A paramilitary wing of the Nazi Party.

SS *Schutzstaffel*, or "Protection Squadron." A paramilitary wing of the Nazi Party.

Treaty of Versailles A treaty between all world powers involved in World War I; it demanded high reparations from Germany that eventually fueled distrust of the government.

vanguard The forefront of change.

FURTHER INFORMATION

Books

Axelrod, Toby. *Hans and Sophie Scholl: German Resisters of the White Rose.* New York: Rosen Publishing Group, 2001.

Freedman, Russell. *We Will Not Be Silent: The White Rose Student Resistance Movement That Defied Adolf Hitler.* New York: Clarion Books, 2016.

Jens, Inge, ed. *At the Heart of the White Rose: Letters and Diaries of Hans and Sophie Scholl.* Walden, NY: Plough Publishing House, 2017.

Nagorski, Andrew. *Hitlerland: American Eyewitnesses to the Nazi Rise to Power.* New York: Simon & Schuster, 2013.

Websites

Center for White Rose Studies

http://www.white-rose-studies.org

Read the full text of all White Rose leaflets and explore more information about the movement.

Holocaust Education and Archive Research Team

http://www.holocaustresearchproject.org

Read information about Adolf Hitler, his government, and resistance movements, including the White Rose movement.

United States Holocaust Memorial Museum

http://www.ushmm.org

Learn more about the terrible toll of the Holocaust through photos, an encyclopedia, and more.

Videos

"The History of Hatred: The Katz Ehrenthal Collection"

https://www.youtube.com/watch?v=R1h3NO9nU2s

A curator from the United States Holocaust Memorial Museum explains the role that antisemitica (art and objects that depict Jews according to hateful stereotypes) played in Hitler's strategy.

"How Did Hitler Rise to Power?"

https://www.youtube.com/watch?v=jFICRFKtAc4

Alex Gendler and Anthony Hazard explain the conditions following World War I that led to Hitler's rise.

BIBLIOGRAPHY

Burns, Lucy. "White Rose: The Germans Who Tried to Topple Hitler." BBC, February 22, 2013. http://www.bbc.com/news/magazine-21521060.

Feuer, Hermann, trans. "Holocaust Research and Archive Education Team: White Rose Leaflets." 2007. http://www.holocaustresearchproject.org/revolt/wrleaflets.html.

Hanser, Richard. *A Noble Treason*. San Francisco: Ignatius Press, 2012.

Lüpke, Marc von. "Sophie, Hans Scholl Remain Symbols of Resistance." *DW*, February 18, 2013. http://www.dw.com/en/sophie-hans-scholl-remain-symbols-of-resistance/a-16605080.

Newborn, Jud, and Annette Dumbach. *Sophie Scholl and the White Rose*. London, UK: Oneworld Publications, 2007.

Scholl, Inge. *The White Rose: Munich, 1942–1943*. Middletown, CT: Wesleyan University Press, 1983.

Spartacus Educational. "Adolf Hitler." Retrieved March 1, 2017. http://spartacus-educational.com/GERhitler.htm.

——. "Sophie Scholl." Retrieved March 1, 2017. http://spartacus-educational.com/GERschollS.htm.

——. "Christoph Probst." Retrieved March 1, 2017. http://spartacus-educational.com/GERprobst.htm.

Wittenstein, George J. "Memories of the White Rose." The History Place, 1997. http://www.historyplace.com/pointsofview/white-rose1.htm.

INDEX

Page numbers in **boldface** are illustrations. Entries in **boldface** are glossary terms.

ABOUT THE AUTHOR

Bridey Heing is a writer and book critic based in Washington, DC. She holds degrees in political science and international affairs from DePaul University and Washington University in Saint Louis. Her areas of focus are comparative politics and Iranian politics. Her master's thesis explores the evolution of populist politics and democracy in Iran since 1900. She has written about Iranian affairs, women's rights, and art and politics for publications like the *Economist*, *Hyperallergic*, and the *Establishment*. She also writes about literature and film. She enjoys traveling, reading, and exploring Washington's many museums.